DOODLE ART ALLEY

COLORING BOOK • VOLUME 13

Samantha Snyder

ISBN-13: 978-0997102123
ISBN-10: 0997102128

This edition is published by aka Associates.
www.akabooks.com

Doodle Art Alley Books

GREAT NECESSITIES call out GREAT VIRTUES.

Abigail Adams

Doodle Art Alley ©

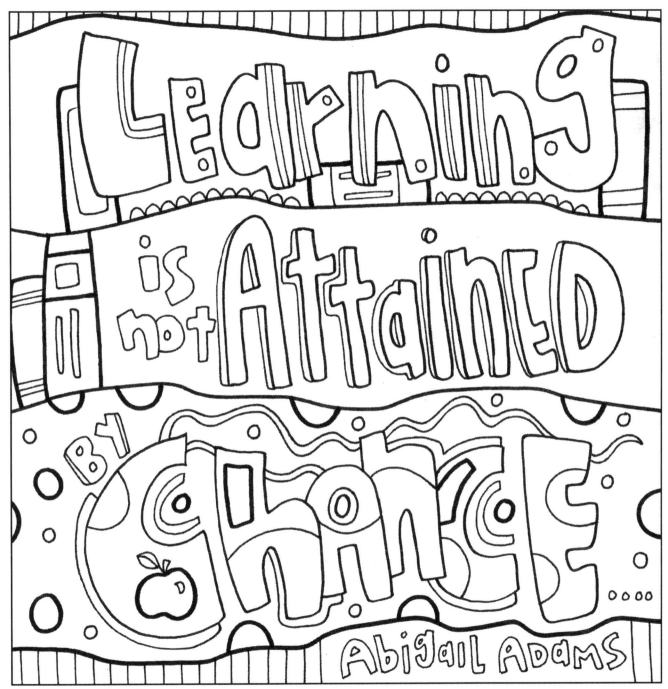

Learning is not Attained by Chance

Abigail Adams

Do the Things you know and you shall learn the Truth you need to know. Louisa May Alcott

Doodle Art Alley ©

I always deserve the best treatment because I never put up with any other.

Jane Austen

Doodle Art Alley

Know your own Happiness.

Jane Austen

Doodle Art Alley ©

It is not easy to be a pioneer but oh, it is fascinating!

Elizabeth Blackwell

None of us can know what we are capable of until we are tested. Elizabeth Blackwell

But he who Dares not Grasp the thorn Should Never Crave the Rose.

Anne Brontë

My Soul is Awakened, My Spirit is Soaring, and Carried aloft on the wings of the breeze.

Anne Brontë

Doodle Art Alley ©

Charlotte Brontë

I am no Bird; and no Net ensnares me: I am a Free human being with an independent will.

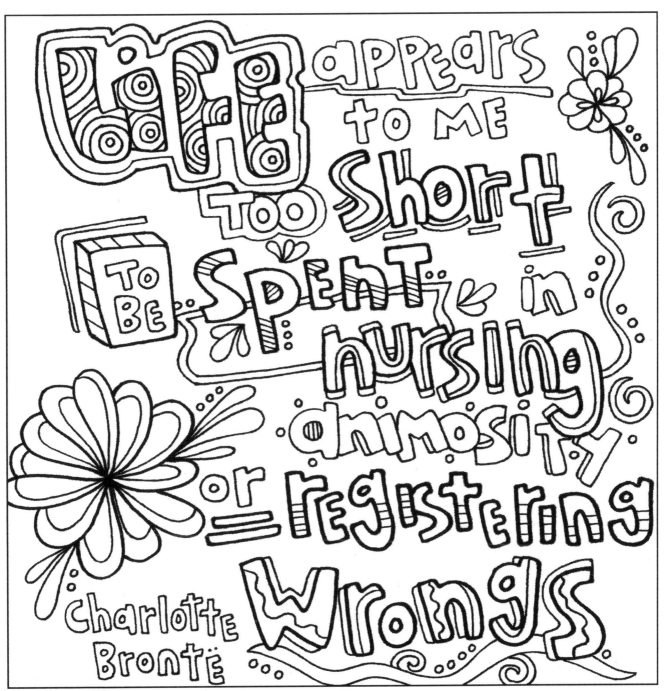

Life appears to me too short to be spent in nursing animosity or registering wrongs

Charlotte Brontë

Doodle Art Alley ©

Elizabeth Barrett Browning

Light Tomorrow With Today.

My Sun Sets To Rise Again

Elizabeth Barrett Browning

Doodle Art Alley ©

Bessie Coleman

I Refused to take NO for an Answer.

The air is the only place free from prejudices. Bessie Coleman

Doodle Art Alley ©

Forever is composed of nows

Emily Dickinson

Hope is the thing with feathers that perches in the soul

Emily Dickinson

I DWELL in POSSIBILITY

Emily Dickinson

Doodle Art Alley ©

I'll Tell You How The Sun Rose, A Ribbon at a Time.

Emily Dickinson

Doodle Art Alley ©

Not Knowing When The Dawn Will Come I Open Every Door.

Emily Dickinson

Truth is Such a rare Thing, It is Delightful to Tell it.

Emily Dickinson

If we take care of the moments, the years will take care of themselves. Maria Edgeworth

Blessed is the Influence of one True Loving Human Soul on Another.

George Eliot

Doodle Art Alley ©

It is Never too Late to be what you might have been.

George Eliot

What do we live for, if it is not to make life less difficult to each other?

George Eliot

Doodle Art Alley ©

A clear and innocent consience fears nothing.

Elizabeth I

A Fool too late bewares when all the peril is past.

Elizabeth I

Mine eyes have seen the glory of the coming of the Lord, He is trampling out the vintage where the grapes of wrath are stored. Julia Ward Howe

Doodle Art Alley ©

Beauty is in the Eye of the Beholder.
Margaret Wolfe Hungerford

All battles are first won or lost in the mind. Joan of Arc

I am not AFRAID I was Born to Do This.

Joan of arc

Life is either a daring adventure, or nothing. Helen Keller

Optimism is the faith that leads to achievement — Helen Keller

Doodle Art Alley ©

He Who Plants a Tree, Plants a Hope.

Lucy Larcom

Doodle Art Alley ©

Doodle Art Alley ©

We too often bind ourselves by authorities rather than by the truth.

Lucretia Mott

Doodle Art Alley ©

No One Can Make You feel Inferior without your consent

Eleanor Roosevelt

Doodle Art Alley ©

The Future belongs to those who believe in the Beauty of their Dreams.

Eleanor Roosevelt

Doodle Art Alley ©

To handle yourself, use your HEAD; to handle others, use your HEART.

Eleanor Roosevelt

With the New Day comes New Strength and new thoughts.

Eleanor Roosevelt

Doodle Art Alley ©

Better by far You Should Forget & Smile Than that You Should Remember and BE SaD. — Christina Rossetti

Christina Rossetti WHO HAS SEEN THE WIND? Neither you & I. BUT when the TREES bow down their HEADS, the WIND is PASSING by.

What is Beautiful is Good, and who is Good will soon be Beautiful. Sappho

I am NEVER afraid of what I know

Anna Sewell

Doodle Art Alley ©

it is good people who make good places

Anna Sewell

Doodle Art Alley ©

The Best.... Protection any woman can have is courage. Elizabeth Cady Stanton

Doodle Art Alley ©

Never give up, for that is just the place and time that the tide will turn.

Harriet Beecher Stowe

Doodle Art Alley ©

Doodle Art Alley ©

Truth is Powerful (and it Prevails.

Sojourner Truth

Doodle Art Alley ©

Every Great Dream begins with a Dreamer. Harriet Tubman

Ella Wheeler Wilcox

Day's Sweetest Moments are at Dawn.

Portraits in Independence

Abigail Adams
November 11, 1744 ~ October 28, 1818

Abigail Adams was the wife of John Adams, the first Vice President and second President of the United States, and the mother of John Quincy Adams, the sixth President of the United States.

She is known for her March 31, 1776 letter to John Adams requesting him to "Remember the Ladies, and be more generous and favourable to them than your ancestors. Do not put such unlimited power into the hands of the Husbands. Remember all Men would be tyrants if they could. If perticuliar care and attention is not paid to the Laidies we are determined to foment a Rebelion, and will not hold ourselves bound by any Laws in which we have no voice, or Representation."

While First Lady, Adams took an active role in both politics and policy. She was an advocate for married women's property rights and for more opportunities for women—especially in the field of education.

Louisa May Alcott
November 29, 1832 ~ March 6, 1888

Louisa May Alcott was an American writer best known as the author of the classic novel *Little Women.* The book has become one of the best-loved books of all time and has been called "the very best of books to reach the hearts of the young of any age from six to sixty."

Raised in New England, Alcott grew up among many of the well-known intellectuals of the day, including Ralph Waldo Emerson, Nathaniel Hawthorne, and Henry David Thoreau, who were family friends.

Alcott was an advocate for women's suffrage and was the first woman to register to vote in Concord, Massachusetts.

Susan B. Anthony
February 15, 1820 ~ March 13, 1906

Susan B. Anthony was an activist, abolitionist, and social reformer who was committed to social equality. She played a pivotal role in the women's rights movement in the United States. In 1867, along with activist Elizabeth Cady Stanton, she founded the American

Equal Rights Association, which campaigned for equal rights for both women and African Americans. The two went on to found the National Woman Suffrage Association in 1869.

Susan traveled extensively, delivering as many as 75 to 100 speeches per year on women's rights. She appeared 40 times before Congress from 1869 to 1906, the year of her death, to ask for passage of a woman's suffrage amendment. The 19th Amendment was finally ratified in 1920, 14 years after her death.

In 1979, in recognition of her dedication and tireless work, the U.S. Treasury Department placed her portrait on the dollar coin, making Susan B. Anthony the first actual woman to be depicted on a circulating U.S. coin.

Jane Austen
December 16, 1775 ~ July 18, 1817

Jane Austen was an English author. Her six novels are considered literary classics, bridging the gap between romance and realism. *Sense and Sensibility*, *Pride and Prejudice*, *Mansfield Park*, and *Emma* were published between 1811 and 1815, and her novels *Northanger Abbey* and *Persuasion* were published in 1818, after her death.

Although not widely known in her own time, Austen's satirical novels of love gained popularity after 1869, and her reputation soared in the 20th century, earning her a place as one of the most widely read writers in English literature. Her books have been adapted numerous times as feature films and television movies and miniseries.

Isabella Beeton

March 12, 1836 ~ February 6, 1865

Isabella Mary Beeton, also known as Mrs. Beeton, was an English author, editor, and journalist.

A magazine journalist working side by side with her publisher husband, Beeton was best known as editor of the wildly popular *Mrs Beeton's Book of Household Management*, a massive guide to running a Victorian household. While it offered advice on a broad range of topics such as frugality, etiquette, fashion, childcare, and the management of servants, most of the book was devoted to cookery. It was illustrated with many colored engravings and was the first cookbook featuring recipes set in the format still used today. Published in 1861, it was expanded multiple times over the years, translated into several languages, and still remains in print.

Elizabeth Blackwell

February 3, 1821 ~ May 31, 1910

Elizabeth Blackwell was a British-born physician, author, and educator. She was the first woman to graduate from medical school in the United States as well as the first woman on the U.K. Medical Register. She became a leading public health reformer during her lifetime.

Blackwell was a pioneer in promoting the education of women in medicine in the United States. In 1857 she cofounded the New York Infirmary for Women and Children. This institution, along with its medical college that opened in 1867, provided training and experience for women doctors and medical care for the poor.

Anne Brontë

January 17, 1820 ~ May 28, 1849

Anne Brontë was an English novelist and poet and the youngest member of the Brontë literary family. Her poetry and her novels were first published under the pen name Acton Bell.

She published a volume of poetry, *Poems by Currer, Ellis, and Acton Bell,* with her sisters, Charlotte and Emily. Her first novel, *Agnes Grey*, was published in 1846. Her second and final novel, *The Tenant of Wildfell Hall*, released in 1848, is considered to be one of the first feminist novels. Her novels, like those of her sisters, have become classics of English literature.

Charlotte Brontë
April 21, 1816 ~ March 31, 1855

Charlotte Brontë was an English novelist and poet, the eldest of the three literary Brontë sisters. Her written works were originally published under the pen name Currer Bell.

Published in 1847, Brontë's best-known novel is *Jane Eyre*, a strong narrative of a woman in conflict that established a platform for feminist writing in the 19th century. This classic continues to be a staple in English literature studies, with Brontë known as one of the most famous Victorian writers.

Elizabeth Barrett Browning
March 6, 1806 ~ June 29, 1861

Elizabeth Barrett Browning was an English poet. Her fourth collection of poetry, titled simply *Poems*, brought her great success and attracted the attention of fellow poet Robert Browning, who became her husband two years later. Her work had a major influence on prominent writers of the day, including American poets Edgar Allan Poe and Emily Dickinson.

Browning's "Sonnets from the Portuguese," one of the most famous collections of English love lyrics, is generally considered to be her best work and most enduring literary achievement. Among the most prominent poets of the Romantic Movement in the Victorian era, she is also admired for the courage of her outspoken views on issues of social injustice.

Bessie Coleman
January 26, 1892 ~ April 30, 1926

Bessie Coleman was an American civil aviator and a pioneer of women in the field of aviation. She was the first woman of African American and Native American descent to be awarded an international pilot's license, and the first to stage a public flight in the United States.

Coleman was known as *Queen Bess* for her successful career in exhibition flying, which ended in 1926 when she died in a plane crash while testing her new aircraft. Her dream of a flying school for African Americans became a reality in 1929 when the Bessie Coleman Aero Club was established in California. In 1995, the U.S. Postal Service issued a Bessie Coleman stamp commemorating "her singular accomplishment in becoming the world's first African American pilot and, by definition, an American legend."

Emily Dickinson
December 10, 1830 ~ May 15, 1886

Emily Dickinson was an American poet. Although extremely prolific in her writings, she was not publicly recognized during her lifetime. After her death, her younger sister, Lavinia, discovered 40 hand-bound volumes of nearly 1,800 poems. The first volume of her work was published in 1890, but it wasn't until 1955 that a complete collection of her poetry was prepared by Thomas H. Johnson for publication by Harvard University Press as *The Poems of Emily Dickinson*.

Known for using unorthodox punctuation, rhythm, and syntax throughout her poetry, Dickinson didn't follow the traditional rules of the genre. She is considered to be one of the most significant American poets of all time.

Maria Edgeworth
January 1, 1768 ~ May 22, 1849

Maria Edgeworth was an Anglo-Irish author and educator known for her children's stories and her novels on Irish life. Her first novel, *Castle Rackrent*, is said to have established the genre of the "regional novel" and was greatly influential. The leading woman novelist of the early 19th century, she counted writers Jane Austen and Sir Walter Scott among her admirers.

A prominent intellectual in Irish history, Edgeworth was a renowned advocate of women's education and held views on estate management and politics that were considered advanced for women of her day.

George Eliot
November 22, 1819 ~ December 22, 1880

George Eliot was the pen name of Mary Anne Evans, an English novelist, poet, journalist, translator, and among the best of the writers of the Victorian era.

Eliot wrote seven acclaimed novels, including *Adam Bede*, *The Mill on the Floss*, *Silas Marner*, and *Daniel Deronda*. Her novel *Middlemarch* has been described as one of the greatest literary works ever written.

Elizabeth I
September 7, 1533 ~ March 24, 1603

Elizabeth I was Queen of England and Ireland. The daughter of King Henry VIII and his second wife, Anne Boleyn, Elizabeth was only the third queen to rule England in her own right, successfully doing so for over 44 years until her death. She was the last monarch of the Tudor dynasty.

Her reign is known as the Elizabethan era. During that period, England flourished as a major European power in politics, commerce, and particularly the arts. Playwrights William Shakespeare, Christopher Marlowe, and many others created plays that transformed theatre in England in that era.

Mary Fields
c. 1832 ~ 1914

Mary Fields was also known as *Stagecoach Mary*. She was the first African-American woman contract mail carrier to deliver U.S. mail. She earned her nickname pushing through bitter weather and over rugged Montana terrain by horse and wagon to deliver important parcels and letters to remote miner's cabins and other outposts. Although she never received formal recognition, her efforts are said to have helped greatly to advance the development of a considerable portion of central Montana.

Born a slave in Tennessee, Fields made her way to Montana in 1884, following the Civil War. For nearly a decade, she lived with the Ursuline nuns at St. Peter's Mission, doing the kind of heavy work typically done by men as well as hauling freight and supplies. In 1902, following her years as a mail carrier, she opened a laundry in Cascade, where she lived until her death, held in high esteem by the locals despite her many eccentricities.

Elizabeth Gaskell
September 29, 1810 ~ November 12, 1865

Elizabeth Gaskell, often referred to as simply Mrs. Gaskell, was an English novelist and short-story writer during the Victorian era.

Her first novel, *Mary Barton*, was published anonymously in 1848 to immediate acclaim, earning praise from Charles Dickens, among others. In addition to her popular novels, Gaskell is known for her book *The Life of Charlotte Brontë*, the biography she penned about her friend Charlotte at the request of Brontë's father after her death.

Julia Ward Howe

May 27, 1819 ~ October 17, 1910

Julia Ward Howe was an American poet, playwright, and book author. Many of her writings reflected her strong beliefs, and from midlife until her death she focused her activities on advancing the causes of women's suffrage, abolitionism, pacifism, and women's education. Howe founded and led several women's organizations and launched the weekly *Woman's Journal*, a suffragist magazine that she contributed to for 20 years. In 1908, Howe became the first woman to be inducted into the American Academy of Arts and Letters.

Howe is best known for writing "The Battle Hymn of the Republic." After hearing an infantry battalion sing the fighting song "John Brown's Body" outside Washington, D.C., she was encouraged by a friend to write new lyrics for the song. Howe claimed the lyrics came to her as she awoke in the early-morning hours of November 18, 1861, when she transcribed them before dawn. The lyrics were first published on the front page of *The Atlantic Monthly* in February 1862. Once set to the music of "John Brown's Body," it became one of the most popular songs of the Union during the Civil War and continues to be a beloved patriotic American anthem today.

Margaret Wolfe Hungerford
April 27, 1855 ~ January 24, 1897

Margaret Wolfe Hungerford was an Irish author of light romantic fiction who wrote under the name "The Duchess."

At least 57 works are attributed to her name and she may have written many more, since much of her earlier work was released anonymously. She is best known for her second novel, *Molly Bawn,* which brought her to fame.

Joan of Arc
January 6, 1412 ~ May 30, 1431

Joan of Arc, also known as "the Maid of Orléans," was a military leader and saint who at the age of 18 led the French army to victory over the English at Orléans during the Hundred Years' War.

Born a peasant, as a child she claimed to have received direction from God to save France by conquering its enemies and installing Charles VII as its king. She convinced Charles to allow her to lead the army to Orléans, where they emerged victorious. After French forces under her guidance took over more enemy territory, Charles VII was crowned king. During a subsequent battle, Joan was captured and imprisoned for several months by English allies. She was put on trial by the English, convicted of heresy, and burned at the stake.

Twenty-five years after her death, a new trial was ordered and her name was cleared of all wrongdoing, with her earlier conviction declared null on the basis of corruption and false charges. Long considered a national hero and a symbol of great courage, Joan of Arc was canonized as a Roman Catholic saint on May 16, 1920.

Helen Keller

June 27, 1880 ~ June 1, 1968

Helen Keller was an American author, lecturer, and political activist. At 19 months old, she suffered an illness that left her deaf and blind. Five years later, her parents located a teacher, Anne Sullivan, who helped Keller overcome her disabilities and learn to communicate. Sullivan remained a mentor and companion to Keller and continued to assist in her education, which ultimately included earning a degree from Radcliffe College, the first college degree earned by a deaf and blind person.

Keller's first book, *The Story of My Life*, detailed her journey from childhood to college student. Her life was depicted numerous times in various forms of media. The best known was *The Miracle Worker*, a dramatic work based on Keller's autobiography first as a teleplay in 1957, then a Broadway play in 1959, and finally an Academy Award-winning feature film in 1962.

Keller went on to devote her life to speaking worldwide and working on behalf of others living with disabilities. She also advocated for women's suffrage, pacifism, labor rights, and other social causes. In 1915 she co-founded Helen Keller International, which focused on research in vision, health, and nutrition. In 1920, she helped found the American Civil Liberties Union. President Lyndon B. Johnson awarded her the Presidential Medal of Freedom in 1962.

Lucy Larcom
March 5, 1824 ~ April 17, 1893

Lucy Larcom was an American poet, abolitionist, and teacher. Her poems appeared in many prestigious journals and magazines, and several collections of her poetry were published as books. Larcom's best-known work, however, is her autobiography, *A New England Girlhood*, released in 1889 and still in print today. The book tells the story of her youth and her years as a textile mill worker from ages 11 to 21, and is a richly detailed account of gender, labor, and class in mid-19th century New England.

Although Larcom never became wealthy, her ability to support herself through writing was unusual for an unmarried woman of her era. Her legacy is honored in a variety of ways: a literary journal, her high-school library, a dormitory at the college where she taught, a park in the mill town where she worked, and even a mountain in an area she frequented all carry her name.

Emma Lazarus
July 22, 1849 ~ November 19, 1887

Emma Lazarus was one of the first high-profile, successful Jewish American authors. She began writing poetry and translating German poems at an early age. Her first commercially published poetry collection, *Poems and Translations,* gained the attention of Ralph Waldo Emerson, among others.

Later in life, Lazarus spoke out against the persecution of Jews in Russia, through both poetry and prose. She became an advocate for Jewish refugees and for the creation of a Jewish homeland. She is best remembered for her sonnet *The New Colossus*, commemorating the plight of immigrants. Its lines were inscribed on a plaque in the pedestal of the Statue of Liberty in 1903.

Lucretia Mott
January 3, 1793 ~ November 11, 1880

Lucretia Mott was an American Quaker, abolitionist, women's rights activist, and social reformer.

A member of the Quaker ministry, she had strong anti-slavery views. Mott helped to found the Philadelphia Female Anti-Slavery Society in 1833 and served as its president. In 1840, when she and the other women delegates were denied participation in the World's Anti-Slavery Convention in London, her passion for women's rights escalated. She became acquainted with activist Elizabeth Cady Stanton at the convention and in 1848 joined Cady Stanton in organizing the Seneca Falls Convention, the first women's rights convention, in Seneca Falls, New York.

In 1864, Mott helped found Swathmore College, still a leading liberal arts college today. In 1866, following the Civil War, Mott was elected the first president of the American Equal Rights Association, an organization that advocated universal suffrage. For the remainder of her life, she used her inspirational speaking skills to advocate for all disadvantaged and disenfranchised Americans regardless of race and gender.

Eleanor Roosevelt
October 11, 1884 ~ November 7, 1962

Eleanor Roosevelt was an American writer, politician, diplomat, and humanitarian. She served as First Lady of the United States during her husband President Franklin D. Roosevelt's four terms in office, greatly expanding that role through her political activity. She regularly held press conferences, traveled across the country giving frequent lectures, hosted a radio show, and wrote a daily syndicated newspaper column, "My Day," which ran six days a week from 1936 to 1962.

After her husband's death in 1945, Eleanor was appointed the first delegate to the United Nations. In April 1946, she became the first chair of the preliminary UN Commission on Human Rights and oversaw the drafting of the Universal Declaration of Human Rights. She was passionate about numerous causes, including women's issues and the civil rights of African Americans and Japanese Americans. In 1961, President John F. Kennedy appointed her to chair the Commission on the Status of Women, and she held that position until shortly before her death. During her lifetime and after her passing, Eleanor Roosevelt was the recipient of numerous awards for her tireless work, including one of the United Nations' first Human Rights Prizes.

Betsy Ross
January 1, 1752 ~ January 30, 1836

Betsy Ross, born Elizabeth Griscom, was a seamstress and American folk hero widely credited with making the first American flag. The story, first made public by her grandson, William Canby, nearly 50 years after her passing, was published in *Harper's Monthly* in 1873. Ross reportedly made the flag in June of 1776 after a visit from General George Washington regarding a design for a flag for the new nation.

Canby relied on family oral history for the tale, and scholars have found no historical evidence that it was actually Ross who made the first flag. However, she was indeed a flagmaker who, records show, was paid in 1777 by the Pennsylvania State Navy Board for making flags. Ross survived three husbands and continued her upholstery and flag-making business for over five decades.

Christina Rossetti
December 5, 1830 ~ December 29, 1894

Christina Rossetti was an English poet who wrote a variety of romantic, devotional, and children's poems. Her best-known works are *Goblin Market and Other Poems* and *The Prince's Progress and Other Poems,* which both featured illustrations by her brother, artist/poet Dante Gabriel Rossetti. These collections established her as a significant Victorian poet. Of her subsequent books, *Sing-Song: a Nursery Rhyme Book* is most notable among children's books of the 19th century.

Interest in Rossetti's writing endures today, and she is considered alongside Elizabeth Barrett Browning as one of the finest women poets of the era.

Sappho
c. 620 BC ~ 550 BC

Sappho was a Greek lyric poet. Her poems were first collected into nine volumes—actually papyrus scrolls—a few hundred years after her death, but by the Middle Ages, nearly all her work had been lost. Out of the roughly 10,000 lines of poetry that collection is estimated to have held, only one 28-line poem of hers has survived in its entirety. Beyond that, all that was left was a handful of lines quoted later by Greek and Roman authors.

A little over 100 years ago, papyrus fragments of her poems began surfacing, and continue to be discovered and catalogued. Sappho's poetry has been described as deeply moving personal reflections on romantic love, desire, and loss. In ancient times Sappho was considered one of the greatest of poets and was sometimes referred to as "The Poetess," much like Homer was called "The Poet." Plato is said to have declared her "the tenth Muse," and her image has been memorialized on coins and in statuary.

Anna Sewell
March 30, 1820 ~ April 25, 1878

Anna Sewell was an English author whose only published work was the classic children's novel *Black Beauty*. Although she had helped edit manuscripts of her mother's books in her youth, she did not become a published author herself until the age of 57.

Sewell wrote *Black Beauty* during the last seven years of her life, when her declining health kept her confined to her home. She had a great love of horses and concern for their humane treatment. In conceiving the book, she explained "a special aim was to induce kindness, sympathy, and an understanding treatment of horses." The book was published just five months before Sewell's death in 1878 and became one of the best-loved children's classics of all time.

Elizabeth Cady Stanton
November 12, 1815 ~ October 26, 1902

Elizabeth Cady Stanton was an American social activist and abolitionist. She was a leading figure of the early women's rights movement.

In 1848, along with Lucretia Mott, Cady Stanton helped organize the Seneca Falls Convention, the first women's rights convention. In 1863, she and Susan B. Anthony formed the Women's National Loyal League, the principal force behind the drive for the Thirteenth Amendment, which abolished slavery. Six years later, the pair created the National Woman Suffrage Association, the precursor to the organization that eventually secured the Nineteenth Amendment, granting women the right to vote.

Beyond women's suffrage, Cady Stanton was an advocate for women's parental and custody rights, property rights, employment and income rights, divorce laws, and birth control. Because of her ardent support of those then-controversial causes, she lost standing among her fellow women reformers. Still, Cady Stanton is credited for being a tireless leader who helped formulate the agenda for woman's rights that has guided the movement to the present.

Harriet Beecher Stowe
June 14, 1811 ~ July 1, 1896

Harriet Beecher Stowe was an American author, abolitionist, and philanthropist. She received national attention in 1852 for her anti-slavery novel, *Uncle Tom's Cabin*. While well-received in the North, the book and its author provoked hostility in the South. It ultimately became a best-seller in the United States, Britain, Europe, and Asia and was translated into over 60 languages.

Stowe was invited to speak about her influential novel and slavery in cities across North America and Europe. She continued to be a successful and prolific writer, completing 30 books over the course of her lifelong writing career.

Jane Taylor
September 23,1783 ~ April 13,1824

Jane Taylor was an English poet and novelist. Taylor and her sister and frequent collaborator Ann Taylor were two of the earliest known children's poets. Her most famous piece was "The Star," more commonly known as "Twinkle, Twinkle, Little Star," which first appeared in 1805 in *Rhymes for the Nursery*, a collection of poems by the Taylor sisters. Her poem was set to an old French tune, creating one of the world's most recognized children's lullabies.

Taylor continued to write poetry, novels, essays, and articles for the remainder of her life. Following her death at age 40, her brother Isaac collected many of her works in *The Writings of Jane Taylor, In Five Volumes,* released in 1832.

Sojourner Truth
c. 1797 ~ November 26, 1883

Sojourner Truth was an African-American abolitionist, speaker, and women's rights activist. She was born into slavery as Isabella Baumfree, but escaped with her infant daughter in 1826.

It was in 1843 when Baumfree changed her name to Sojourner Truth, and subsequently dedicated her life to the abolition of slavery. In 1851 She delivered her best-known speech on racial inequality, "Ain't I a Woman?," at the Ohio Women's Rights Convention. During the Civil War, Truth helped recruit black troops for the Union Army. For the remainder of her life, she continued to speak fervently on women's rights, universal suffrage, and prison reform.

Harriet Tubman
c. 1822 ~ March 10, 1913

Harriet Tubman was an African-American abolitionist and humanitarian. Born into slavery, Tubman escaped with her infant daughter, Sophia, in 1827 and courageously made numerous missions to rescue approximately 70 enslaved family members and friends through the network known as the Underground Railroad.

She offered her services to the Union Army during the Civil War, working as nurse, spy, and scout. Tubman was the first woman to lead an armed expedition in the war when she led 150 black Union soldiers in the Combahee River Raid, which liberated more than 750 slaves in South Carolina.

After the war ended, Tubman dedicated her life to helping impoverished former slaves and the elderly, establishing a Home for the Aged, which became her own residence in 1911, two years before her death.

Ella Wheeler Wilcox
November 5, 1850 ~ October 30, 1919

Ella Wheeler Wilcox was an American author and poet whose early poems were published while she was still in high school. Her most famous poem, "Solitude," was first published in the February 25, 1883 issue of *The New York Sun*. The poem was included in her collection *Poems of Passion* shortly after.

Though not critically acclaimed, Wilcox's poetry was widely known and well loved by the general public. Her cheerful and optimistic themes were expressed in plainly written rhyming verse, many lines of which became enduring, popular quotes.

ABOUT DOODLE ART ALLEY

Samantha Snyder has been doodling her whole life. While teaching elementary school, she often drew up coloring pages and printables for her students and fellow teachers. She decided to start sharing her creations and in 2008,
Doodle Art Alley was founded.

A quick glance at a doodle may show scribbles, random lines and shapes with no meaning or significance. However, with a little love and direction, these drawings have the potential to compete with some of the best artwork there is!

Doodle Art Alley is dedicated to giving those squiggly lines the proper credit they deserve. Who would have thought that such a small and simple idea could possess so much potential?

There are lots of fun doodle art activities, tips, and information to read through and enjoy. Visit www.doodle-art-alley.com for hundreds of exciting doodles.

Doodle Art Alley Books

Made in the USA
San Bernardino, CA
01 April 2017